Starter Book 2

The tunes in Level 1 used these sounds

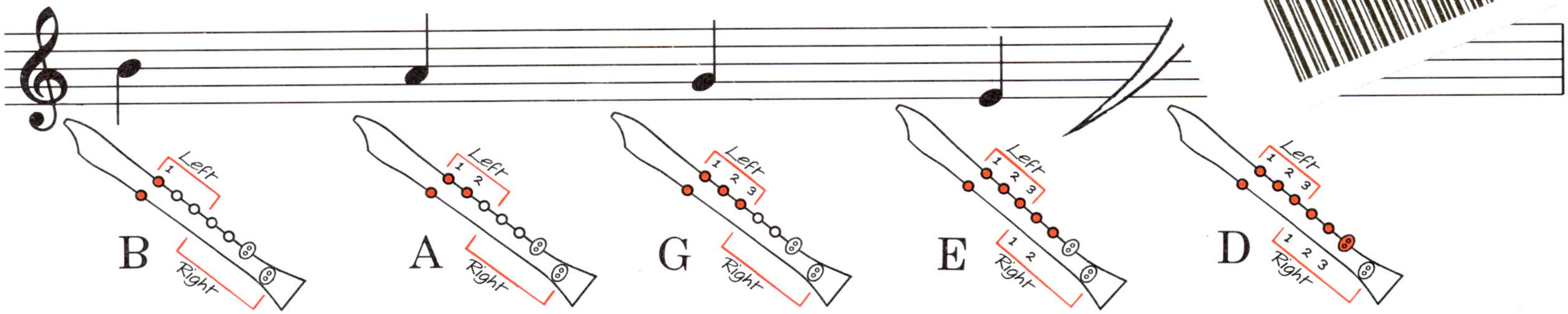

The tunes in $\frac{2}{4}$ $\frac{3}{4}$ and $\frac{4}{4}$ used

walking notes
or crotchets
lasting 1 beat

running notes
or quavers lasting
$\frac{1}{2}$ beat each

crotchet rests
for
1 beat silence

The tunes in $\frac{6}{8}$ used

step-skip beats
made up of
a crotchet
and a quaver

or steps
made up of
a crotchet
with a quaver rest

Slurs and sirens

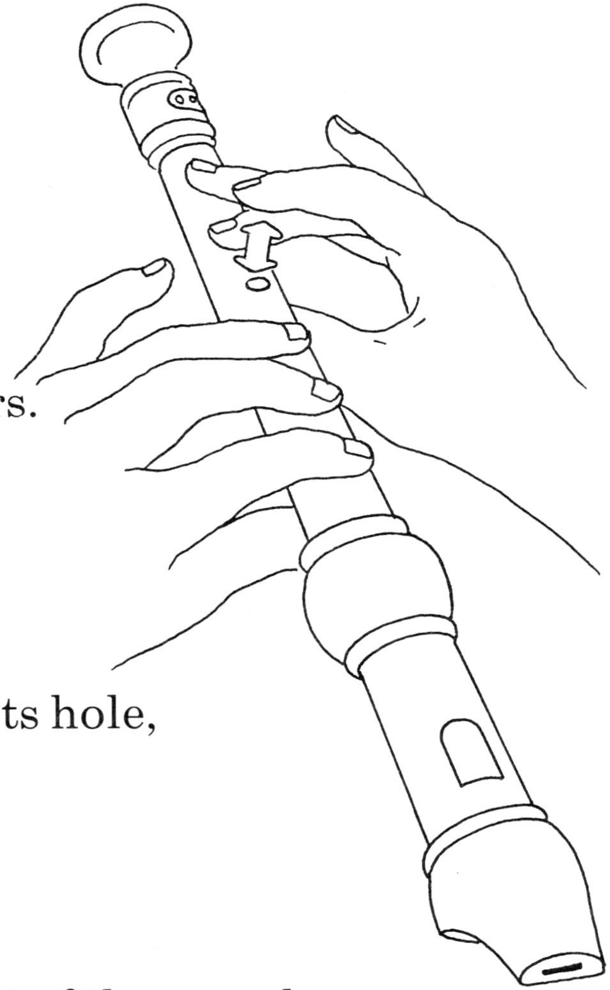

Pick me up with both hands.
Cover the thumb-hole,
and three finger-holes with **each** hand,
ready to play the note D.
Remember, left hand nearest my lip and yours.
Now blow through me a smooth and long
tooooooooooooooooooooooooooooooooooooo
Keep the tone steady.

Now blow again, only this time
lift your **right-hand first finger** on and off its hole,
making a sound like a siren.

tooooo oooooo oooooo oooooo oooooo oooooo

Notice you only say ‘t’, or tongue, at the start of the sound.

When you join up notes like this you **slur** them.
The sound you joined with D was **F sharp**.

F♯

To play F sharp, cover the holes as for the note D but lift up the first finger of the right hand, like this:

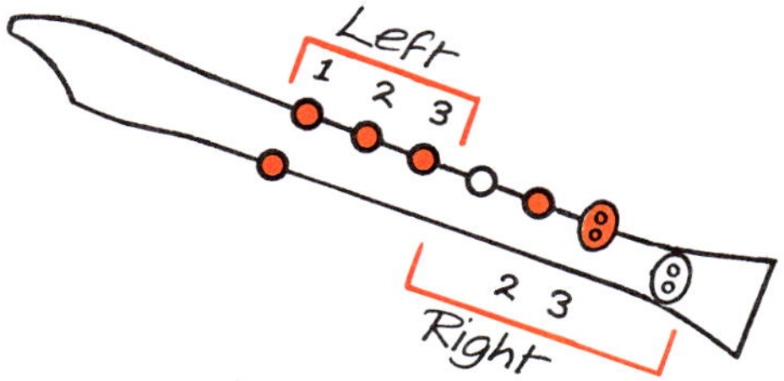

To write F sharp, put a note in the bottom space and write a sharp sign in front of it:

Slur Mix

Just like D and F♯, other sounds can be

tongued

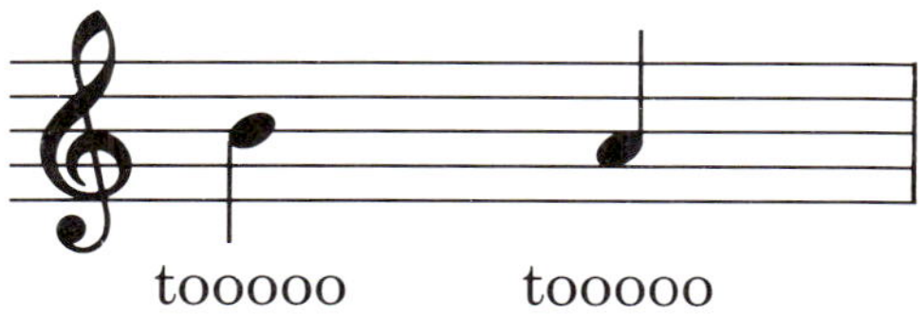

or slurred

Here are some more groups

to tongue

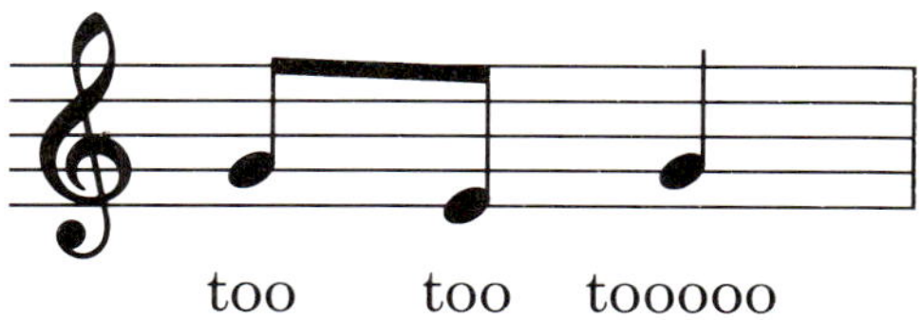

or slur

Mix them together to make tunes like this:

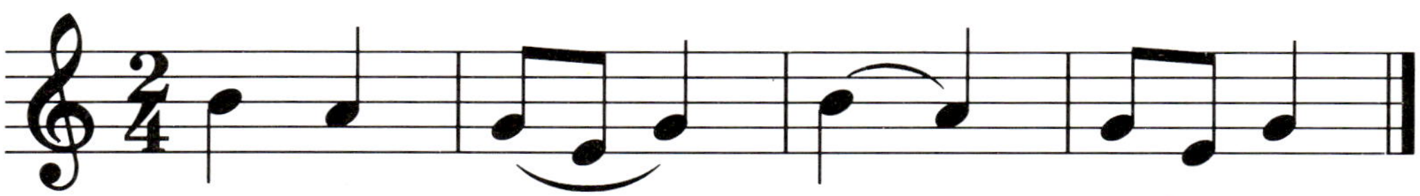

On my hat

Key of G

Tunes with F♯ often end on G. They are in the key of G.

To show this, a sharp sign is written on the top line of the stave, like this:

This is called a key signature.

The top line of the stave is also F.

Au clair de la lune

French traditional tune

There's a hole in my bucket

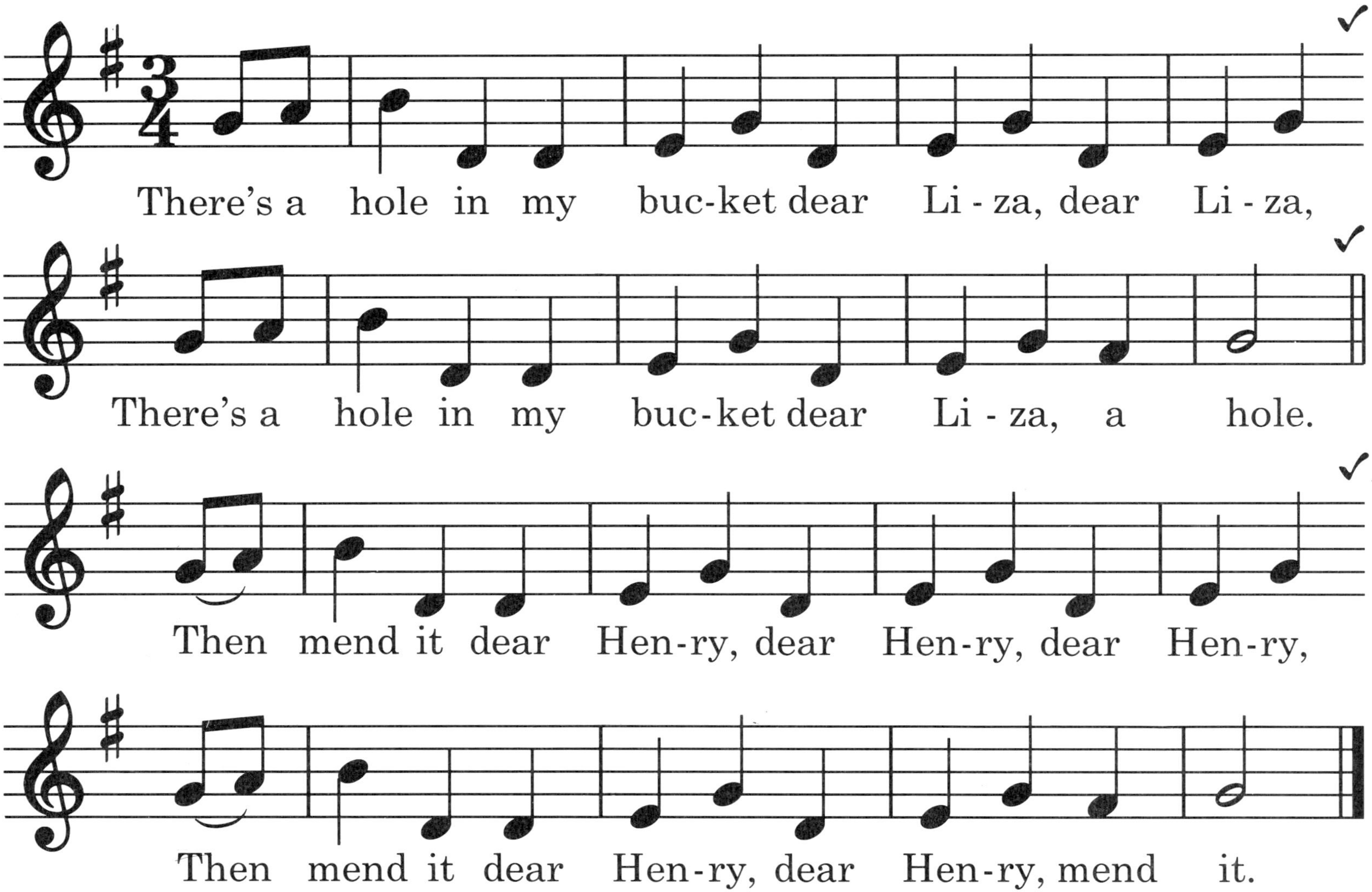

We've got a wheeliebin

Based on the traditional British tune 'Dance to Your Daddy'

C´

To play top C, (which we label C′), cover the thumb-hole, and the second hole, like this:

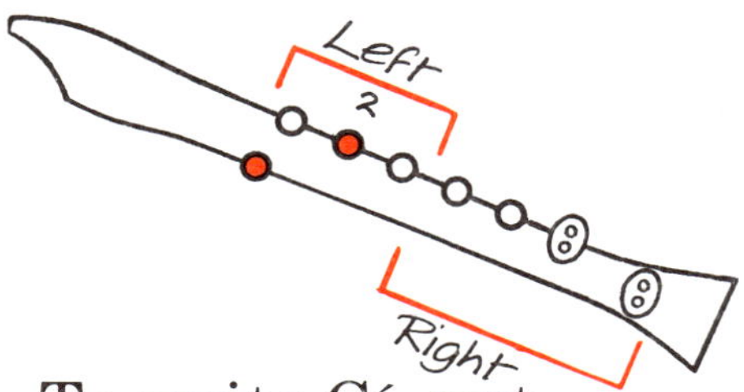

To write C´, put a note in the space above the middle line, like this:

Word Mix

Can you remember the B A G tune and the E G G tune?
Here they are:

Now that you know some more notes you will be able to think up other 'word tunes' to mix together.

Here are some ideas to get you going:

And some other words to turn into music:

BAGGAGE FEED CAFE CADGE BEEF

Pease pudding hot

Traditional English

I like baked beans

Hush little baby

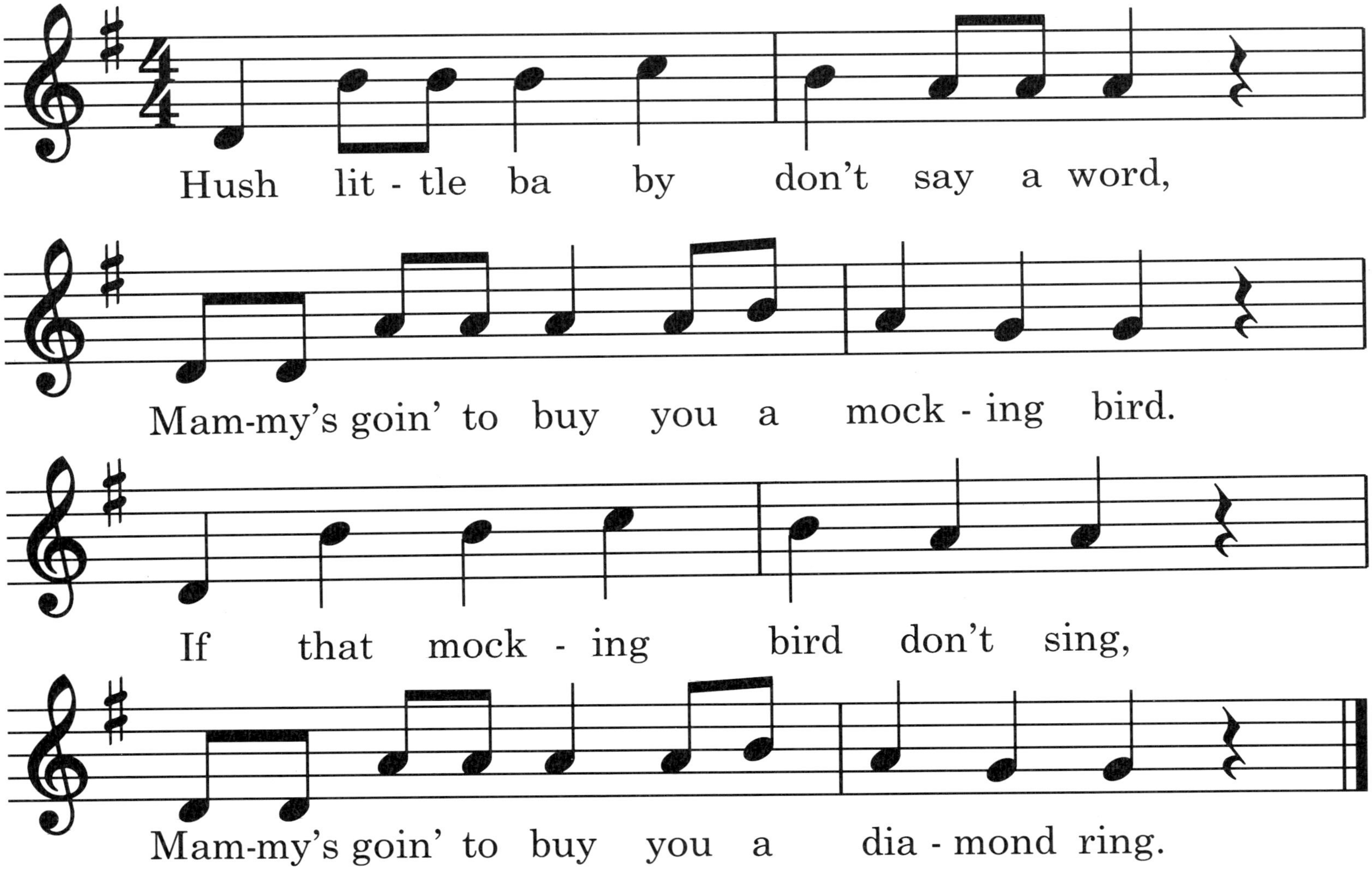

Traditional American

The CABBAGE Patch

How many cabbages are there in this patch?

D´

To play top D (which we label D´), finger the note C´, and then lift off the thumb at the back, like this:

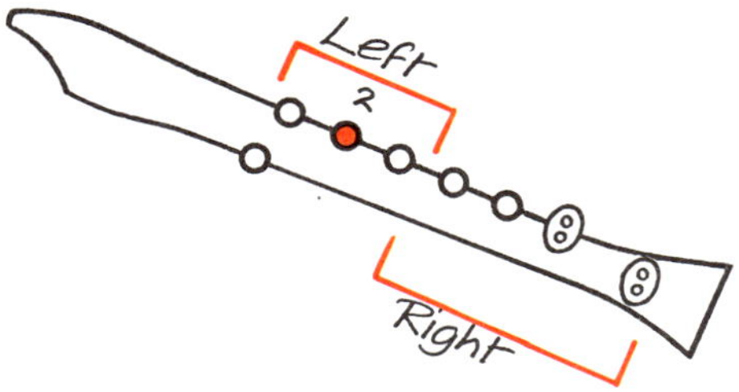

To write D´, put a note on the fourth line up, like this:

Snakes and Ladders Mix

Here is a musical ladder from G to D´. Play up it a step at a time:

Here is another ladder from D to A:

Mix these ladders with little snakes

toooooooooooo

toooooooooooo

or long curly snakes

to make up your own snakes and ladders tunes.

Go tell Aunt Nancy

American folk song

Green and white

German folk song

This is how I slip and slide

Three gentlemen

Traditional French

Three sad seals

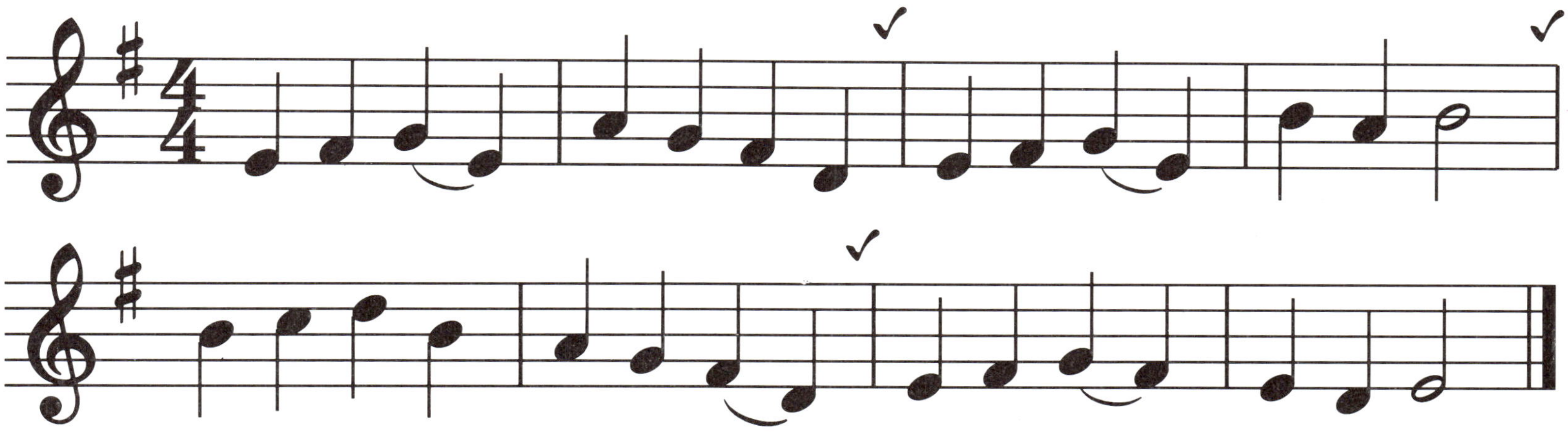

Praise God from whom all blessings flow

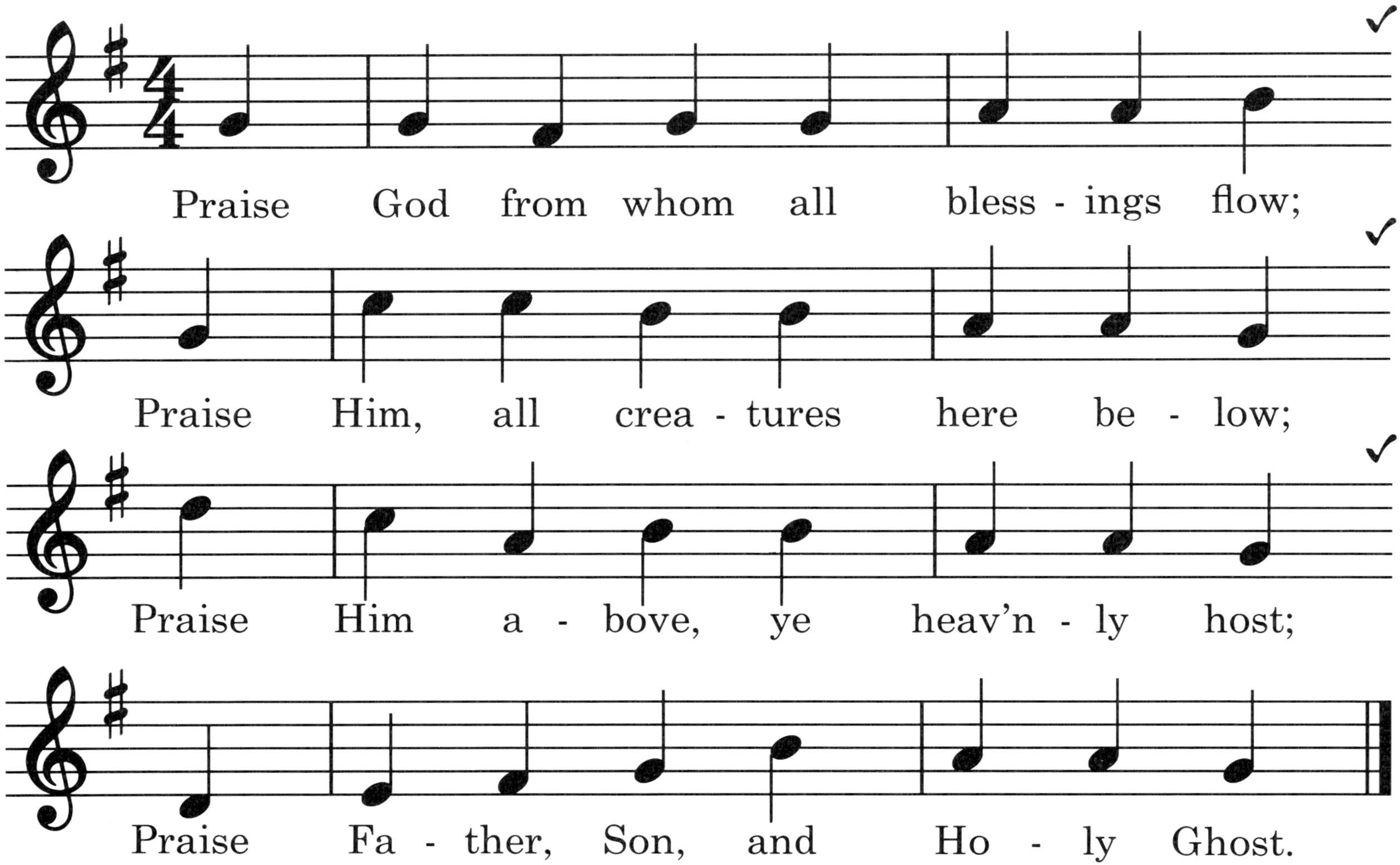

'Tallis's Canon'

Tickety, tackety, tickety tack

C♯´

C sharp sounds a half-step higher than C. To play top C ♯, finger the note A but lift off the thumb at the back, like this:

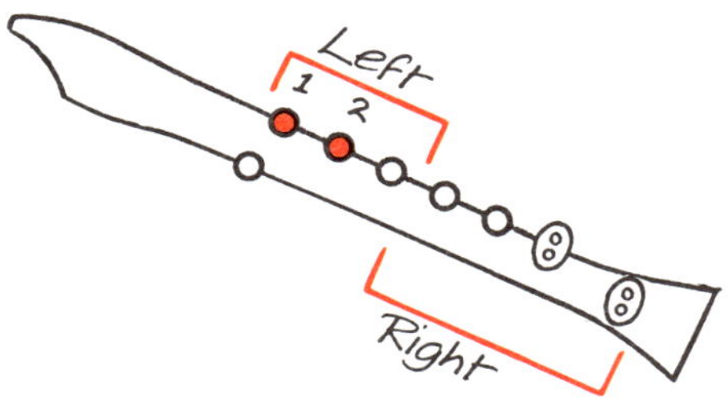

To write C sharp, put a sharp sign in front of C, like this:

Thumb Twister Mix

A tongue twister is tricky to say.
A thumb twister might be tricky to play.
These thumb twisters mix the notes
A and C´ (thumb-hole closed) with
C ♯´ and D´ (thumb-hole open).

As with tongue twisters, practise them again and again until you can play them well.

1

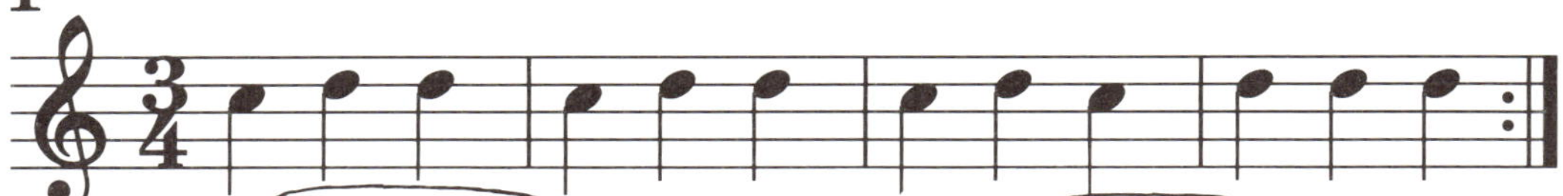

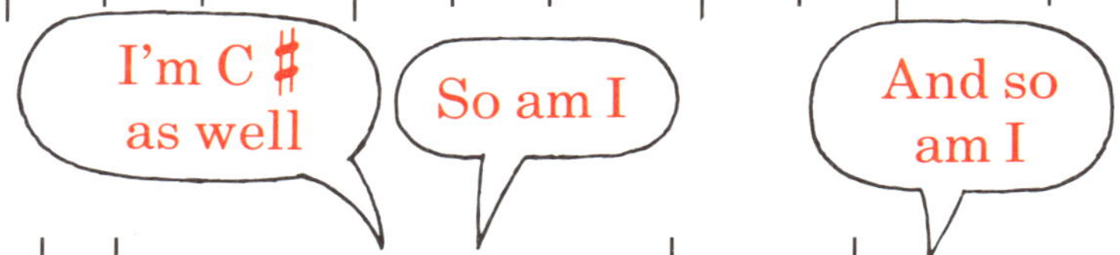

2

3

This thumb twister changes time as well:

Can you make up some more thumb twisters with these notes?

Sharp Ahead!

Key of D

Tunes which use C♯ often end on D. They are in the key of D. To show this, add C♯ to the key signature, like this:

Chocker whacker, chocker whacker, great big ball

One little brown bird

Traditional

Try adding this second part to the tune above.
Except in one place the rhythm is the same.
Can you see where that is?

Dickory Dock

Traditional